rockschool®

Piano Debut

Performance pieces, technical exercises, supporting tests and in-depth guidance for Rockschool assessments

All accompanying and supporting audio can be downloaded from: *www.rslawards.com/downloads*

Input the following code when prompted: **VXNL8A4UT2**

For more information, turn to page 5

Acknowledgements

Published by Rockschool Ltd. © 2019 & 2020
Catalogue Number: RSK200089US
ISBN: 978-1-78936-165-0
Initial US Release | Errata details can be found at *www.rslawards.com/errata*

SYLLABUS
Syllabus designed and written by Jono Harrison
Syllabus Director: Tim Bennett-Hart
Syllabus consultants: Gary Sanctuary, Chris Stanbury, Simon Troup and Jennie Troup
Hit Tune arrangements by Jono Harrison and Gary Sanctuary
Supporting Tests written by Jono Harrison, Chris Stanbury, Nik Preston and Ash Preston
Syllabus advisors: Tim Bennett-Hart, Brian Ashworth, Stuart Slater, Peter Huntington, Bruce Darlington, Simon Troup and Jennie Troup

PUBLISHING
Proof reading of arrangements by Sharon Kelly, Simon Troup, Jennie Troup and Jono Harrison
Music engraving and book layout by Simon and Jennie Troup of Digital Music Art
Fact files written and edited by Abbie Thomas
Notes written by Roland Perrin
Proof reading and copy editing by Gemma Bull, Jono Harrison and Jennie Troup
Cover design by Philip Millard of Rather Nice Design
Cover photograph: © Nomad_Soul (Shutterstock)

AUDIO
Produced by Jono Harrison
Engineered by Jono Harrison, Gary Sanctuary, Tim Bennett-Hart, Pete Riley, Richard Brook, Rory Harvey and Andy Robertson
Assisted by Paul Pritchard at Abbey Road
Recorded at Dock Street Studios, The Dairy and Abbey Road
Mixed by Patrick Phillips
Mastered by Francis Gorini

Supporting Tests recorded by Chris Stanbury and Jono Harrison

MUSICIANS
Piano and Keyboards: Jono Harrison, Gary Sanctuary, Ross Stanley & Tania Ilyashova
Piano on 'Imagine': Charlie Connell
Drums & Percussion: Pete Riley and Richard Brook
Bass & Synth Bass: Andy Robertson
Guitars: Rory Harvey, Nat Martin and Jono Harrison
Saxophone: Jonathan Griffiths
Trombone: Tom George White and Norton York
Trumpet: Nick Mead and John Simpson
Lead and Backing Vocals: Glen Harvey & Katie Hector
Additional Programming: Jono Harrison

DISTRIBUTION
Exclusive Distributors: Hal Leonard

CONTACTING ROCKSCHOOL
www.rslawards.com
Telephone: +44 (0)345 460 4747
Email: *info@rslawards.com*

EXECUTIVE PRODUCERS
John Simpson, Norton York

Awarding the Contemporary Arts

Table of Contents

Introductions & Information

Rockschool Level/Grade Pieces

Technical Exercises

Supporting Tests

Additional Information

Welcome to Rockschool Piano Debut

Welcome to Rockschool's Piano syllabus 2019. This syllabus is designed to support pianists in their progression from Debut to Level/Grade 8, through an engaging and rigorous pathway covering all the genres, stylistic elements, techniques and musical skills required for success as a contemporary pianist.

Piano Assessments

At each level/grade you have the option of taking one of two different types of assessment:

- Level/**Grade Assessment**
  A Level/Grade Assessment is a mixture of music performances, technical work and tests. You are required to prepare three pieces (two of which may be Free Choice Pieces) and the contents of the Technical Exercise section. This accounts for 75% of the assessment marks. The other 25% consists of: either a Sight Reading or an Improvisation & Interpretation test (10%), two Ear Tests (10%), and finally you will be asked five General Musicianship Questions (5%). The pass mark is 60%.

- **Performance Certificate**
  A Performance Certificate is equivalent to a Level/Grade Assessment, but in a Performance Certificate you are required to perform five pieces. A maximum of three of these can be Free Choice Pieces. Each song is marked out of 20 and the pass mark is 60%.

All elements required to participate in a Rockschool assessment can be found in the level/grade book. These are as follows:

- **Assessment Pieces**
  The 2019 syllabus comprises six 'hit tune' arrangements, benchmarked and devised so as to equip contemporary pianists with industry-relevant skills in any performance environment. These fall into three categories:

  Melody & Accompaniment
  These arrangements are performed to full band backing tracks, with the piano performing both melody and accompaniment

  Solo Piano Arrangement
  These are full solo piano arrangements, performed without backing tracks

  Vocal Accompaniment
  These arrangements cover the skills required of contemporary pianists in ensemble environments, be they on the stage or in the studio. The backing tracks feature vocalists, and the piano parts are reflective of what session pianists would perform live or on mainstream commercial recordings

  Each 'hit tune' arrangement is preceded by a Fact File, giving surrounding context to the piece and the original performers/recording artists.

  Furthermore, at the end of each arrangement you will find notes giving additional supportive context to get the most out of the pieces.

- **Technical Exercises**
  There are either three or four groups of technical exercise, depending on the level/grade:

  Debut–Level/Grade 8:
  Group A: Scales
  Group B: Arpeggios/Broken Chords
  Group C: Chord Voicings

  Levels/Grades 4–8 only:
  Group D: Technical Study

- **Supporting Tests**
  There are three types of unprepared supporting tests in the assessment:

  1. The first type can be one of two options (this is the *candidate's* choice):

     Either:
     Sight Reading tests, developing the musician's ability to read and perform previously unseen material;

     or:
     Improvisation & Interpretation tests, developing the musician's ability to develop previously unseen material in a stylistic way and perform improvised passages of melody. The book contains examples of both types of test – equivalent 'unseen' examples will be provided for the assessment

  2. **Ear Tests**
     Debut–Level/Grade 3: feature Melodic Recall and Chord Recognition
     Levels/Grades 4–8: feature Melodic Recall and Harmonic Recall

  3. **General Musicianship Questions (GMQs)**, which you will be asked by the assessor at the end of each assessment

General Information

You will find information on assessment procedures, including online assessment entry, marking schemes, information on Free Choice Pieces and improvisation requirements for each level/grade.

Audio

In addition to the level/grade book, we have also provided audio in the form of backing tracks (minus piano) and full tracks (including piano) for all 'hit tune' arrangements, technical exercises and supporting tests (where applicable). We have provided professional performance recordings of all solo piano pieces in the syllabus. This audio can be downloaded from RSL directly at *www.rslawards.com/downloads*

You will need to input this code when prompted: **VXNL8A4UT2**

The audio files are supplied in MP3 format. Once downloaded you will be able to play them on any compatible device.

Further Information

You can find further details about Rockschool's Contemporary Piano syllabus by downloading the syllabus guide from our website: *www.rslawards.com*

All candidates should download and read the accompanying syllabus guide when using this level/grade book.

Performance and Technical Guidance

Fingering
Any fingering annotation is given as a guide only.

Interpretation
Notation should be performed exactly as written, except where there are performance indications to ad. lib, improvise, develop, etc. In these instances, the candidate will be marked on their ability to interpret the music in a stylistically appropriate way, commensurate with the level.

Adaptation
A small degree of adaptation is allowed where, for example, hand stretches do not facilitate the required notated parts. Marks may be deducted if adaptation results in over-simplification of the notation. If in doubt you can submit any adaptation enquiries to *info@rslawards.com*

Articulation & Dynamics
Where articulation and dynamics are marked on the notation, they should be followed. Where it is open to interpretation, the candidate is free to take their own approach.

Pedalling
The candidate may use the pedal freely at any level/grade, but it should be applied judiciously as marks may be deducted for any over usage resulting in an unclear tone. In addition, where pedalling is written into (or out of) the notation, this should be observed.

Chord Symbols
Most hit tune arrangements have chord symbols written above the notation. This is purely for guidance, and to assist the candidate and teacher.

Next to Me

SONG TITLE:	'NEXT TO ME'
ALBUM:	OUR VERSION OF EVENTS
RELEASED:	2012
LABEL:	VIRGIN
GENRE:	R&B/SOUL/GOSPEL
WRITTEN BY:	EMELI SANDÉ/HUGO CHEGWIN/ HARRY CRAZE/ANUP PAUL
PRODUCED BY:	CRAZE & HOAX/MOJAM MUSIC
US CHART PEAK:	25

British singer songwriter Emeli Sandé released her single 'Next to Me' in 2012, the third to be released from her debut album *Our Version of Events*. The track was originally released in Ireland where it topped the charts, it was then released in the UK shortly after and peaked at number two. 'Next to Me' hit the US Billboard charts in April of 2012 and gave Sandé her first US top 40, peaking at number 25. The song is listed as the 14th best selling single of 2012 in the UK, a brilliant achievement for the singer songwriter.

Emeli Sandé received positive feedback for the hit, with many reviewers left wondering if the "morally righteous" man she refers to in her lyric is in fact a partner. Listeners may well construe that she is referring to her faith, or maybe even music itself. In 2013 the song made an appearance in an episode of US Musical Sitcom Glee and was performed by Rachel Berry and none other than Broadway star Idina Menzel. Here the pair sing a harmony led arrangement and keep Sandé's gospel feel very much alive in the song.

Born Adele Emily Sandé in 1987 and raised in Aberdeenshire, Sandé showed a keen interest in music and songwriting from an incredibly young age. She wrote her first song at the age of 11 and immediately knew that music was the path she had to follow. She felt strongly about writing her own material, rather than performing songs written by others, and found it to be a natural talent. In 2009 she collaborated with rapper Chipmunk on his track 'Diamond Rings'. The song achieved top 10 status on the UK charts and led to many more musical ventures for Sandé.

In 2011 she released her first solo single 'Heaven' and shortly after released her debut studio album *Our Version of Events*. The album was a great success and topped the UK album chart, spending ten consecutive weeks at number 1 and becoming the best selling UK album of 2012. Not stopping there, the album went on to win her British Album of the Year at the 2013 Brit Awards Ceremony. She also won Best British Female Solo artist at the same ceremony, an outstanding accomplishment for such a young singer songwriter.

Long Live the Angels was Sandé's second studio album and peaked at number 2 in the UK album chart (2016). In 2017 she was appointed the prestigious status of MBE for her services to music. Her songwriting and outstanding vocal have clearly left an impact on the UK's music industry, the MBE status is well deserved for such a talented individual.

Next To Me

Emeli Sandé

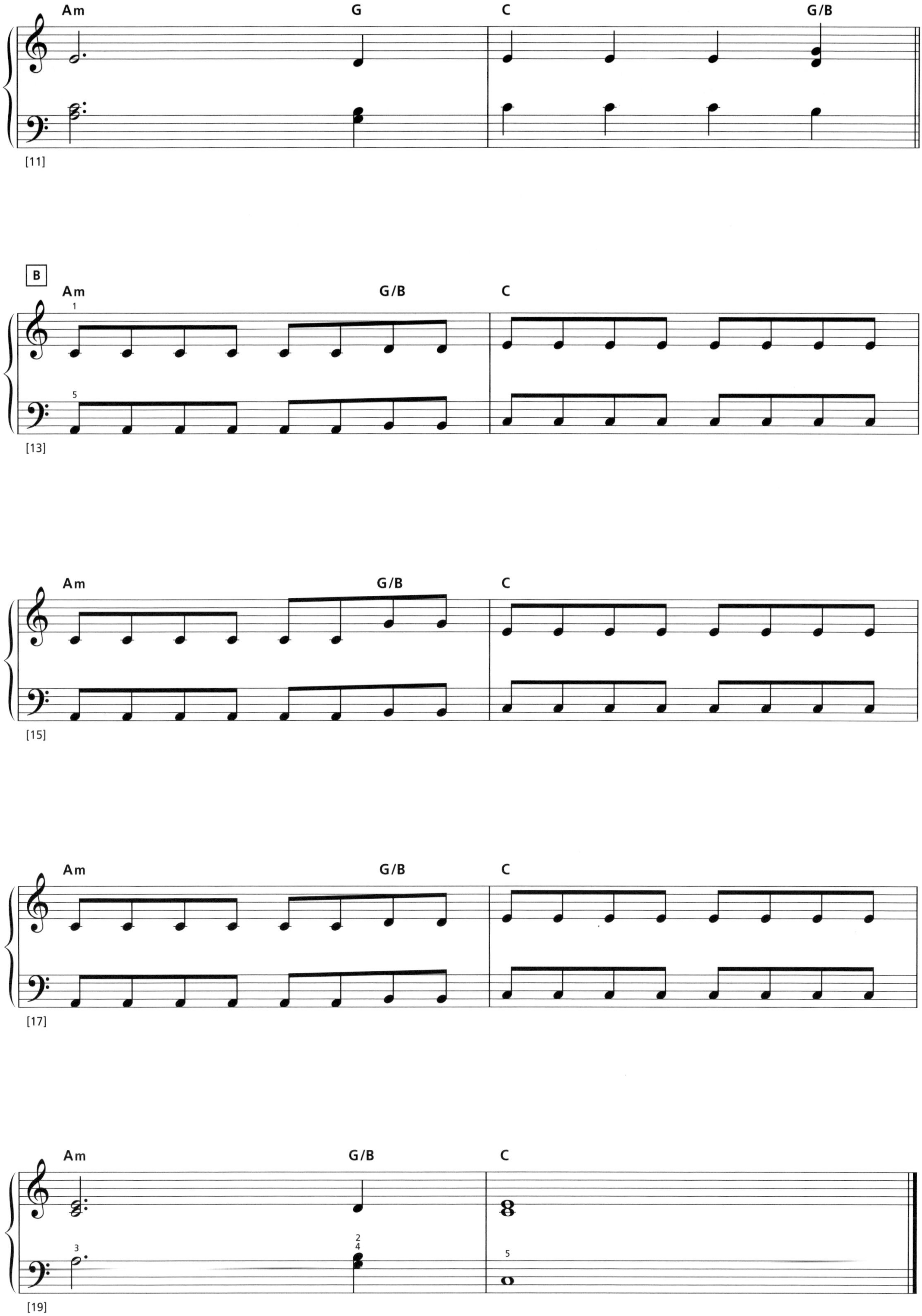
Am
G
C
G/B
[11]
B
Am
G/B
C
[13]
Am
G/B
C
[15]
Am
G/B
C
[17]
Am
G/B
C
[19]

Notes

The lyrics in 'Next To Me' express the value of constancy and friendship, and this sentiment is reflected in the steady pulse and repetitive rhythm of the opening piano chords.

In order to play this passage, it may be helpful to count the beats out loud (1, 2, 3, 4) and then add the eighth notes (1 & 2 & 3 & 4 &). Once comfortable, this should be counted silently. It may help to play this passage with a fairly 'loose' wrist, observing hand position and fingering as the notes move closer together from measure 1 to measure 2.

The verse of the song (A) starts at measure 5 and the chords become sustained, providing a 'bed' for the vocal melody. It is good practice to ensure that all the notes in the chords sound clearly and evenly.

The rhythm builds to quarter notes in measure 12, setting up the chorus (B) at measure 13. Here, the piano part plays the same chords as the introduction, but using different voicings. Care is needed here in the wider separation between the two hands.

Lastly, be sure to hold the final chord for its full length, to the end of the final measure.

Imagine

SONG TITLE: 'IMAGINE'
ALBUM: IMAGINE
RELEASED: 1971
LABEL: APPLE
GENRE: SOFT ROCK/POP
WRITTEN BY: JOHN LENNON/YOKO ONO
PRODUCED BY: JOHN LENNON/YOKO ONO/ PHIL SPECTRE
US CHART PEAK: 3

Written by John Lennon in 1971, 'Imagine' was a worldwide hit which conveyed themes of politics, religion and love. Lennon wrote the song at his home in Berkshire and was heavily influenced by the poetry works of his wife Yoko Ono, specifically her book *Grapefruit*, so much so that she was later given a writing credit. His song speaks of a world where all humans are one, with no countries or religion to separate them. Lennon was often criticised by religious groups, claiming that the song was an atheist anthem. However, Lennon is quoted as stating that the song was not about a world with no religion at all but rather a world of one religion without competition as to whose God is the most powerful. An intriguing sentiment which was well received by the ever-liberal movement of the 1970s.

'Imagine' was released in the US in late 1971 and peaked at number 3 on the Billboard Hot 100 chart. Although the single wasn't officially released in the UK at that time, the LP on which it featured (of the same name) managed to top the UK album charts in the November of that year. It was later released as a single in the UK in 1975 to promote a compilation LP and peaked at a respectable number 6. Re-released for one last time following the Singers tragic death in 1980, 'Imagine' finally achieved the position it deserved and claimed number 1 in the UK Singles Charts.

The song itself has sold over 1.6 million copies in the UK alone, making it by far Lennon's biggest success as a solo artist. He is of course widely known as one part of the multimillion selling quartet, The Beatles. During their time together, The Beatles took the world by storm, shaping the music industry as we know it today an immeasurable amount. To date, The Beatles are the best-selling band of all time, with estimated sales of over 800 million records worldwide.

Following his huge success with The Beatles, Lennon went on to influence countless musicians and was highly regarded in the industry. His song' 'Imagine' was actually inducted into the Rock and Roll Hall of Fame's *500 Songs that Shaped Rock and Roll* and earned him a Grammy Hall of Fame Award. Since it's original release 'Imagine' has been covered by dozens of successful artists, including: Madonna, Stevie Wonder, Elton John, Joan Baez and Diana Ross. It is a fitting tribute to the incredible songwriter that was John Lennon, that so many music icons would want to cover this unquestionably remarkable song.

Imagine

John Lennon

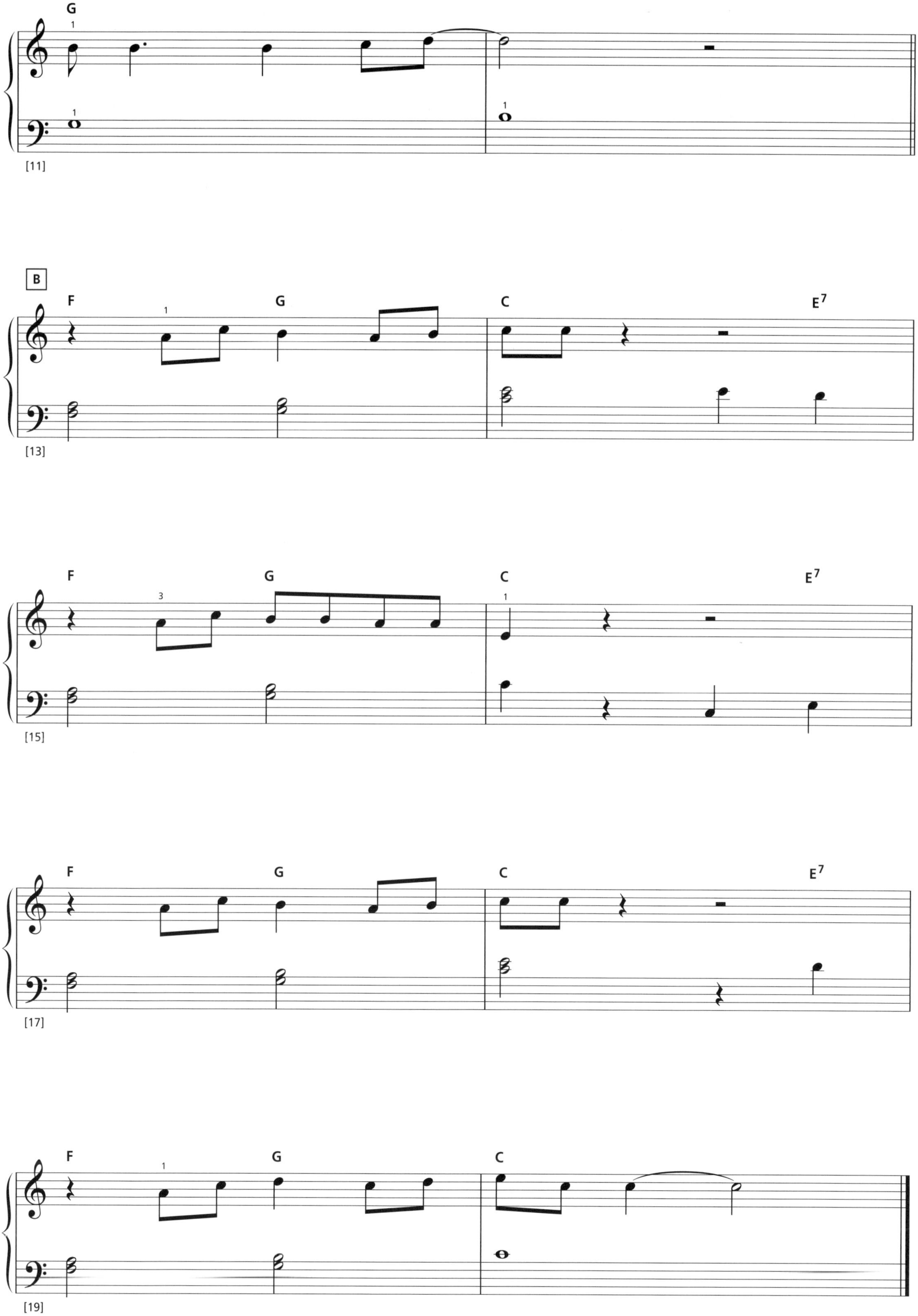
G
[11]
B
F G C E7
[13]
F G C E7
[15]
F G C E7
[17]
F G C
[19]

Notes

'Imagine' features essential melody and accompaniment techniques which, when mastered, provide a good foundation for pop and rock piano styles. The left hand in measures 1–8 outlines the chords, with a single note adding movement to every second measure on the fourth beat. By contrast, the right-hand melody is based around quarter notes and eighth notes, mirroring John Lennon's vocal line. At measure 9, the left hand plays a descending stepwise scale, until two-note chords are reintroduced in the chorus at measure 13.

The right hand melody needs to be played evenly and securely, using five fingered positions where possible. It may also be useful to refer to the fingering guidance on the score. It is important to produce clear chords and bass notes in the left hand, without becoming overpowering.

The rests should be observed carefully in this arrangement, and there should be an awareness of when one of the hands is resting and where both hands are resting. For example, care is needed in measure 2 not to play the first note in the right hand for longer than a quarter note. Also, in measure 10, the third note in the right hand should be shorter than the first note in measure 2. In measure 16, for the first time, both hands are resting, creating a silence in both the accompaniment and the melody.

Lastly, be sure to hold the last notes in both hands until the very end of the final measure.

Beauty And The Beast

SONG TITLE:	'BEAUTY AND THE BEAST'
ALBUM:	BEAUTY AND THE BEAST: ORIGINAL MOTION PICTURE SOUNDTRACK
RELEASED:	1991
LABEL:	WALT DISNEY
GENRE:	SHOW TUNE
WRITTEN BY:	HOWARD ASHMAN/ALAN MENKEN
PRODUCED BY:	HOWARD ASHMAN/ALAN MENKEN
US CHART PEAK:	9

'Beauty and the Beast' was written by lyricist Howard Ashman and composer Alan Menken for Disney's 1991 animated feature film of the same name. Originally recorded by actress Angela Lansbury for her role as the voice of character Mrs. Potts, the song told the story of main characters Belle and the Beast. The song features in the famous ballroom scene, in which the two characters discover for their love for each other despite their differences. A chorale version also features in the final scene of the movie, while themes of the song appear frequently throughout the film's full score.

Having been vacant from the pop charts for over 30 years, Disney saw an opportunity to promote their feature film and popularise their music again. They enlisted the help of Celine Dion (a newcomer at the time) and Peabo Bryson to record a pop version of the theme song. Disney had originally planned to use Dion as a soloist for the recording, but were concerned that her status at the time wasn't big enough to draw attention and so Bryson was brought in to duet. Little did they know that Celine Dion would go on to become a worldwide, multimillion selling artist. Of course, they may well have played a hand in her success by introducing her to the mass market with this iconic theme tune.

Both Lansbury and Dion/Bryson's versions were hugely successful, winning multiple awards including a Golden Globe and Academy Award for Best Original Song, as well as a Grammy Award for Best Song Written for Visual Media. In 2004 the original composition was officially deemed one of the greatest songs in film history by the American Film Institute who ranked it number 62.

'Beauty and the Beast' was again recorded in 2017 by actress Emma Thompson for the character of Mrs Potts. As a homage to Dion and Bryson's beautiful portrayal of the song, Ariana Grande and John Legend recorded a similar duet to be released for the 2017 adaption of 'Beauty and the Beast'.

Disney's original animated feature film, 'Beauty and the Beast' (1991), became the first ever animated film to win the Golden Globe Award for Best Picture – Musical or Comedy. With an original budget of $25 million the animation went on to gross $425 million worldwide and became one of Disney's best selling feature films of all time.

Beauty And The Beast

Alan Menken

From 'Beauty And The Beast' (1991)

C
F
[13]
C
G
[15]
F
C/E
Dm
G
[17]
C
G
[19]
F
C/E
Dm
G
[21]
C
[23]

Notes

There is a serene quality to this song. To reflect this in performance, the notes should be played smoothly and evenly, with the performer being careful not to rush against the pulse.

The melody is performed by the right hand, and needs to be clearly projected over the left hand accompaniment without being too heavy. It is important to observe the rests – these are where the singer would breathe, giving a natural 'shape' to the music.

The fingerings may prove a useful starting point in building stability. Each melodic phrase differs from the last, so a solid fingering technique will ensure confidence.

Be careful to hold the notes in the final two measures for their full duration, noting that the right hand finishes at the end of measure 23 while the left hand notes are tied and held throughout the final measure.

SONG TITLE: LEAN ON ME
ALBUM: STILL BILL
RELEASED: 1972
LABEL: SUSSEX
GENRE: SOUL

VOCALS: BILL WITHERS
PIANO: BILL WITHERS
BASS: MELVIN DUNLAP
DRUMS: JAMES GADSON
ARRANGER: RAYMOND JACKSON

WRITTEN BY: BILL WITHERS
PRODUCED BY: BILL WITHERS
US CHART PEAK: 1

Withers states that he could afford to buy a "little Wurlitzer electric piano" with the proceeds from his first album and it was on this that he composed 'Lean on Me'. As he was playing the piano, the song's title popped into his head and the lyrics developed from there. Withers says that he is a man of few words when writing songs: "snob, lyrically. That means, how clear can you make it and in how few words?"

Withers didn't record his first song until he was 32, having previously worked in the US Navy. When he left the Navy, he started informally writing songs, recording demos and trying to gain interest from record companies. Eventually, he was introduced to Booker T. Jones (of Booker T. and the MGs, the Stax Records house band) who offered to produce his first album, *Just As I Am*, which gave him his way into the record industry. However, he refused to quit his job immediately as he felt the music industry was fickle.

Although the song only reached No. 18 in the UK charts, it peaked at No. 1 in the Billboard Hot 100 in 1972. Withers has won three Grammy awards, one of which was for this song. 'Lean on Me' also featured at the end of an episode of *The Simpsons*.

Interestingly, Bill Withers walked away from the music industry saying that "these days I wouldn't know a pop chart from a Pop-Tart". He has not performed publicly in concert for over 25 years. He is often asked if 'Lean on Me' can be used for TV shows and films but he refuses to have the song synchronised with any violent scenes: "we don't want people to associate 'Lean on Me' with violence". Anyone wishing to use one of his songs has to contact him personally.

This song is often popular with young pianists as the verse can be played without removing your hand from the piano and using the first four fingers on your right hand.

Lean On Me

Bill Withers

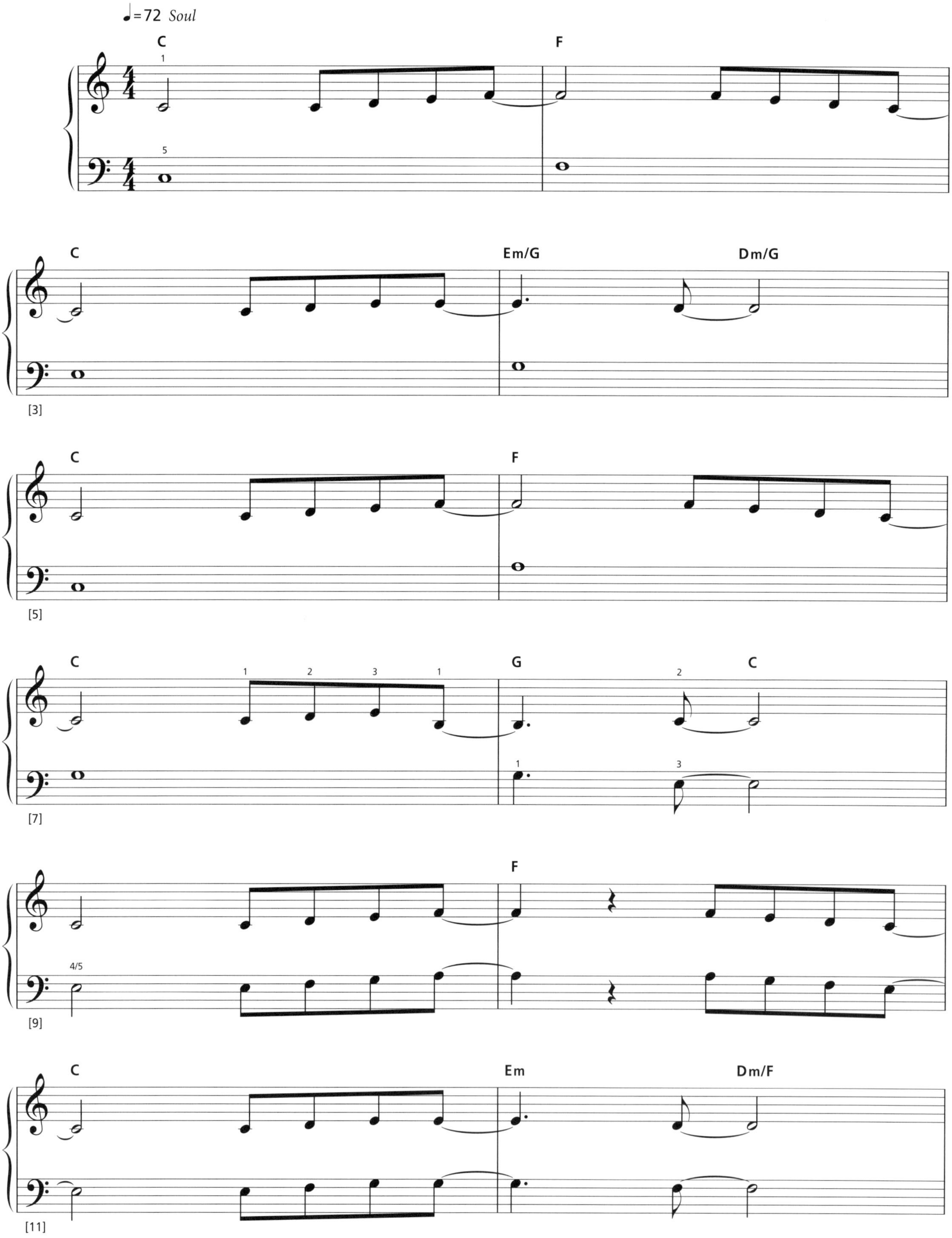

C
F
[13]
C
G
C
[15]
C
F
[17]
C
Em
Dm/F
[19]
C
F
[21]
C
G
C
[23]

Notes

The melodies in this song feature syncopation – a rhythmic feature essential to playing rock and pop music.

The main challenge first appears in the opening two measures, where the right hand phrase ends before the left hand. To master this, it can be effective to omit the tie in the right hand part, and play the 'F' twice – on the and of the fourth beat, and also on the first beat of the second measure. Once this is achieved, include the tie in the right hand.

There are a number of phrases that end with two repeated eighth notes – in measure 3, for example. To achieve an authentic soul feel, the first of these two notes should be shortened and the second one slightly accented.

There is another challenging syncopation in measure 8, where both hands finish on the and of the second beat. It is important to count the third and fourth beats silently as this will help avoid rushing to the next measure.

From measure 9 onwards, the hands have a number of unison syncopations. Again, care is needed with the 'silent' beats – they must be counted, but not played. In measure 10, make sure the rests in both hands are observed.

Measure 16 presents another challenge: the right hand part has to rise from middle 'C' to a high 'E'. Students should practise these two notes very slowly, right hand alone, making sure the fifth finger is above the 'E' before playing it. The note should be approached from above, not from an angle.

Lastly, it is important to count the four beats of the last measure silently in order to make sure that the right hand and left hand finish together.

SONG TITLE: 'LOVE YOURSELF'
ALBUM: PURPOSE
RELEASED: 2015
LABEL: DEF JAM
GENRE: ACOUSTIC POP
WRITTEN BY: ED SHEERAN/BENNY BLANCO/ JUSTIN BIEBER
PRODUCED BY: BENNY BLANCO
US CHART PEAK: 1

'Love Yourself' was a hit for Canadian pop star Justin Bieber, the third single to be released from his fourth studio album *Purpose.* The song became Bieber's third consecutive number one single in both the US and the UK. In total, the single topped the charts in no less than fifteen countries, including; Australia, Canada, Denmark, Portugal, Sweden and Slovakia (to name a few).

'Love Yourself' was written by pop sensation Ed Sheeran, with co-writing credits going to Justin Bieber as well as record producer Benny Blanco. While Bieber tells the tale of an iconic songwriting session with Sheeran, in which they discuss similar experiences and emotions, Sheeran's explanation behind the song is quite different. Originally written for his album *Divide,* Sheeran scrapped the song for his own release and set out to find another artist for whom it may be more suitable. Regardless of which tale is closer to the truth, the song became a global hit achieving 3xPlatinum status in the UK and a staggering 7xPlatinum status in the US.

Having debuted at number three in the UK Singles Chart, it didn't take long for the track to rise to the top spot. Just two weeks after its release 'Love Yourself' took the top spot only to replace another of Bieber's hits, 'Sorry', making him the first artist since 2005 to replace themselves at the top of the charts. With 'Sorry' now in second place, Bieber was holding both number 1 and number 2 in the UK Singles Chart and managed to do so for four consecutive weeks. This was an incredible accomplishment for the young artist, in which he outdid The Beatles record for holding number 1 and number 2 for three consecutive weeks in 1967/1968.

'Love Yourself' was met by a mixture of positive and negative feedback, with most reviewers complimenting the Canadian singer for his simple and stripped back delivery. Many felt that the simple acoustic guitar and trumpet backing helped convey an honest delivery and with Sheeran's lyrics Bieber was able to voice an in-depth story, a technique in which perhaps many of his previous releases had been lacking.

Justin Bieber released his debut album *My World 2.0* in 2010 and since then has become a worldwide household name. Of his four studio album releases, all have reached the top ten in the UK album chart and all have reached number 1 in the US. Having recently taken a break from the music industry, Bieber is now working on his fifth Studio album and we can only expect the same level of success going forward.

Love Yourself

Justin Bieber

B
Am F C Am F C
[18]
Am F C G Am F G
[22]
C
C G Am F C F C
[26]
C G Am F C F C
[30]

Notes

Originally performed on voice and guitar, 'Love Yourself' is an intimate and direct pop song with a slightly melancholy undertone. This will be best reflected in performance with a light touch, *legato* fingering in the right hand and clear projection of the melody. It may help to use the suggested fingering guidelines as a starting point to get into the correct position for each phrase.

It is important to ensure that the right hand and left hand connect rhythmically throughout, and this can be achieved by silently counting the beats in the measure – firstly the quarter note 'down' beats (1, 2, 3, 4) then adding the eighth note 'up' beats (1 & 2 & 3 & 4 &).

The rests play a significant role in the right hand, by creating the natural effect of a vocalist pausing to breathe, whereas in the left they provide textural variety – for example, in measure 4 and measure 8 – as well as help mark the end of sections. From measure 26, it is crucial to observe the rests in the left hand as they give the music more of a groove to the accompaniment.

Lastly, it is important to count right to the end of the final measure before releasing the sustained left hand chord.

La Valse d'Amélie

SONG TITLE: 'LA VALSE D'AMÉLIE'
ALBUM: AMÉLIE
RELEASED: 2001
LABEL: VIRGIN RECORDS
GENRE: AVANT-GARDE/BAL-MUSETTE/ CONTEMPORARY CLASSICAL
WRITTEN BY: YANN TIERSEN
PRODUCED BY: YANN TIERSEN
US CHART PEAK: N/A

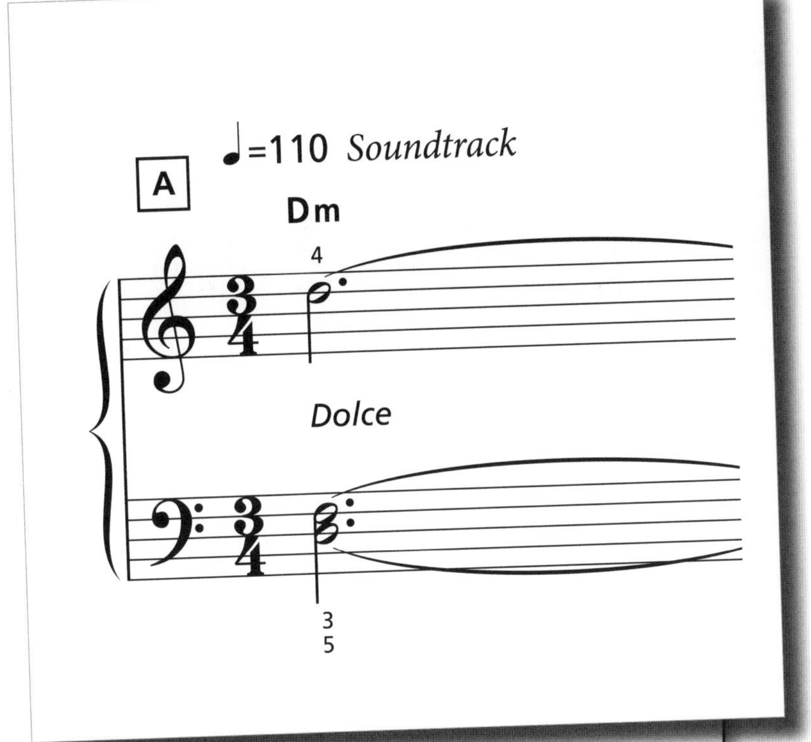

La Valse d'Amélie is taken from Yann Tiersen's award winning soundtrack for the French romantic comedy, Amélie. Tiersen's beautiful composition features on the soundtrack twice, both as an orchestral piece and a piano piece. The composer also included the orchestral version in his fourth studio album, *L'Absente*, shortly after the release of the soundtrack in 2001.

Much like the film, the soundtrack *Amélie* was well received worldwide, topping the charts in its home nation of France as well as the second spot in the US Billboard Top World Music Albums chart. The release was certified Gold in the UK with sales of over 100,000 and 3xPlatinum in France with sales over 900,000. Worldwide sales stand at just over 1.5 million, a number which reflects the regard in which this beautiful soundtrack is held.

Director Jean-Pierre Jeunet happened upon Yann Tiersen's music when a friend played his CD during a car journey they were on together. He had never heard the composer's work before and was immediately intrigued. Jeunet took it upon himself to buy Tiersen's entire catalogue, listening to all of it with admiration for the French composer. The director then approached Tiersen and asked him to compose a soundtrack for his up and coming film 'Amélie', an offer which of course Tiersen was delighted to accept. The soundtrack went on to include some of Tiersen's existing works, taken from his three previous studio albums, as well as pieces written especially for the film. These newly commissioned works include the piece 'La Valse d' Amélie'.

Tiersen won two awards for his soundtrack *Amélie,* in 2001 he took the award for Best Original Score of the Year at the World Soundtrack awards and in 2002 he was awarded Best Music Written for a Film at the César Award ceremony. The release also received nominations for BAFTA's coveted award for Best Film Music in 2001, World Soundtrack's 2001 award for Soundtrack Composer of the Year and Phoenix Film Critics Society Award for Best Original Soundtrack of the Year.

Jean-Pierre Jeunet's adaption of the stunning French tale was also well received, with leading lady Audrey Tautou being praised for her 'lively' and 'delightful' performance. The 2001 film release won several awards, including two BAFTAs at the 2002 ceremony for both Best Original Screenplay and Best Production Design.

La Valse d'Amélie

Yann Tiersen

From Amélie' (2001)

F
C
[25]
F
C
[29]
C
Dm
Am
[33]
Dm
Am
[37]
F
C
[41]
F
C
[45]
D
Dm
Am
[49]

Notes

There is something of a sensitive, child-like innocence to Amelie's character, reflected in the opening four measures with the '*dolce*' indication. Nonetheless, she is intelligent and quietly strong – qualities that can guide the performer's interpretation as the music evolves, repeating melodic themes with alternating rhythmic and chordal ideas.

Written in ¾ time (a 'waltz'), it is important to observe the '*lightly*' indication at letter B. To achieve the 'lilting' effect of this time signature the right hand chords (beats 2 & 3) should have less emphasis than the beat 1 chordal root note in the left hand.

Throughout the piece, the melody needs to be projected clearly over the chords but not too heavily. It can therefore be helpful to think of playing the left hand more quietly, rather than over-emphasising the right, particularly at letter C as the left hand plays single notes.

The final four measures contain left-hand chords only and these should be very light, but with every note in the chord sounding together, clearly and evenly.

Technical Exercises

In this section you will be required to play a selection of exercises drawn from each of the groups below. The assessor will be looking for the speed of your response and will also give credit for the level of your musicality. Please see the syllabus guide for details on the marking criteria.

All scales and arpeggios need to be played hands separately, in straight feel, ascending and descending, in the keys, octaves and tempos shown. Pentatonic scales are right hand only. You may use your book for Group A and Group B. Group C exercises must be played from memory.

Note that Groups A and B need to be played to a click and any fingerings shown are suggestions only.

Group A: Scales
The tempo for this group is ♩= 52 bpm.

1. C major scale | right hand

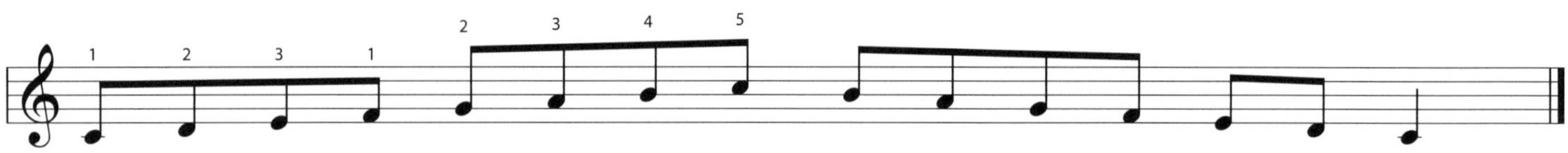

2. C major scale | left hand

3. A natural minor scale | right hand

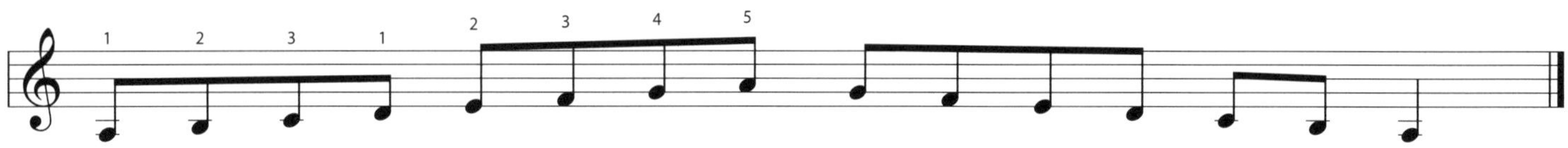

4. A natural minor scale | left hand

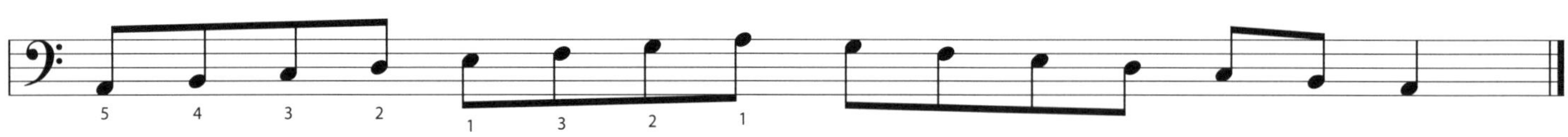

5. C major pentatonic scale | right hand

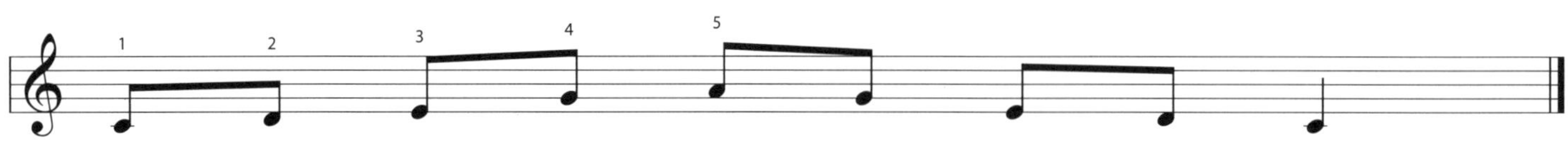

6. A minor pentatonic scale | right hand

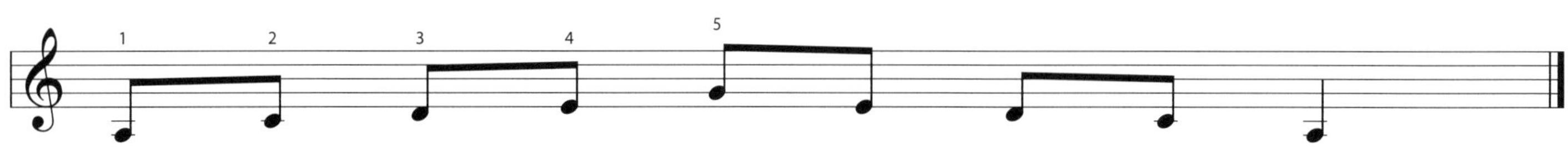

Group B: Arpeggios/Broken Chords

The tempo for this group is ♩=92 bpm.

1. C major broken chord | right hand

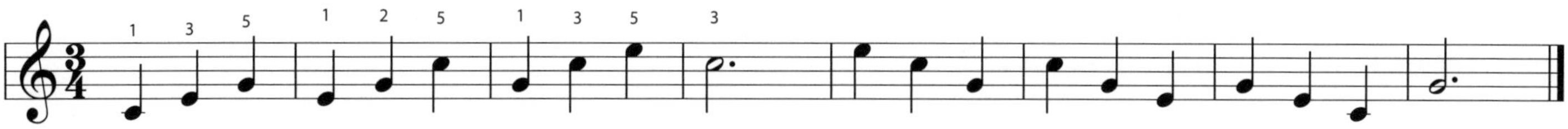

2. C major broken chord | left hand

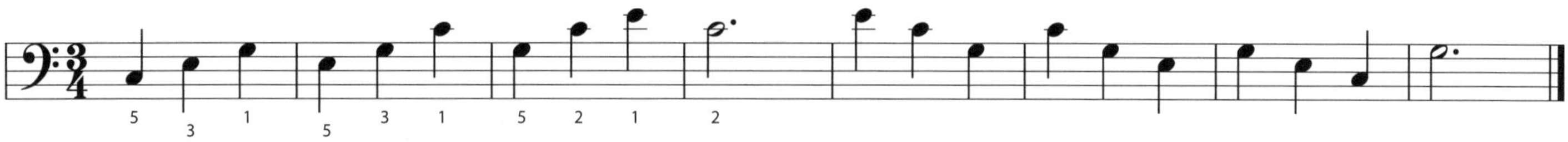

3. A natural minor broken chord | right hand

4. A natural minor broken chord | left hand

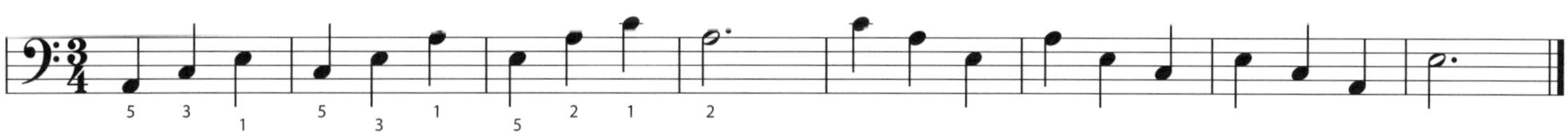

Group C: Chord Voicings

Major and Minor Triads

In the assessment you will be asked to play either the C major voicings or the C minor voicings below, from memory. The assessor will state the exercise and the key. This test is performed in free time (without backing track or click), but the assessor will be looking for the speed of your response.

1. C major

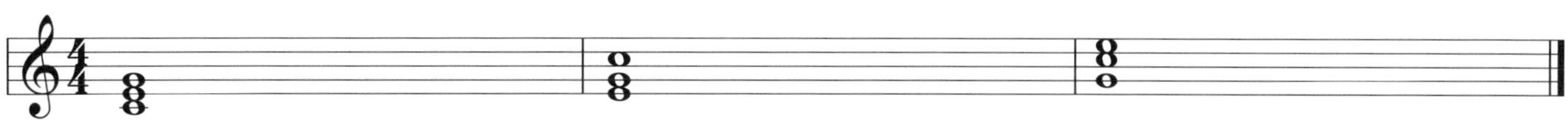

2. C minor

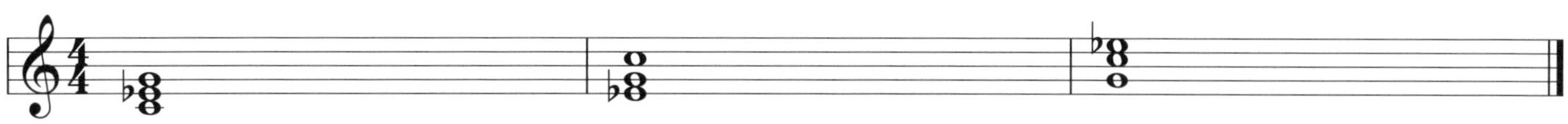

Sight Reading

In the assessment, you have a choice between either a Sight Reading test or an Improvisation & Interpretation test. The assessor will ask you which one you wish to choose before commencing. Once you have decided you cannot change your mind.

In the sight reading test, the assessor will give you a 4–6 measure melody in the key of C major. You will first be given 90 seconds to practise, after which the assessor will play the backing track twice. The first time is for you to practise and the second time is for you to perform the final version for the assessment. For each playthrough, the backing track will begin with a one measure count-in. The tempo is ♩=60.

During the practice time, you will be given the choice of a metronome click throughout or a one-measure count in at the beginning.

The backing track is continuous, so once the first playthrough has finished, the count in of the second playing will start immediately.

Sight Reading | Example 1

Sight Reading | Example 2

Please note: The tests shown are examples: The assessor will give you a different version in the assessment

Improvisation & Interpretation

In the assessment, you have a choice between either a Sight Reading test or an Improvisation & Interpretation test. The assessor will ask you which one you wish to choose before commencing. Once you have decided you cannot change your mind.

In the Improvisation & Interpretation test, the assessor will give you a 4–6 measure chord progression in the key of C major. You will first be given 90 seconds to practise, after which the assessor will play the backing track twice. The first time is for you to practise and the second time is for you to perform the final version for the assessment. For each playthrough, the backing track will begin with a one measure count-in. The tempo is ♩= 60.

During the practice time, you will be given the choice of a metronome click throughout or a one measure count-in at the beginning.

The backing track is continuous, so once the first playthrough has finished, the count-in of the second playing will start immediately.

You are only required to improvise single note melodies, with either right or left hand. It is permissible to play chord voicings, but please note you will only be marked on melodic content.

Please note: The test shown is an example. The assessor will give you a different version in the assessment.

Ear Tests

In this section, there are two ear tests:

- Melodic Recall
- Chord Recognition

You will find one example of each type of test printed below and you will need to perform both of them in the assessment.

Test 1 | Melodic Recall

The assessor will play you two consecutive notes. You will need to identify whether the last note is higher or lower than the first. You will hear the test twice, each time with a one measure count-in. The tempo is ♩=95 bpm.

For this exercise, please use the word 'higher' or 'lower' in your answer.

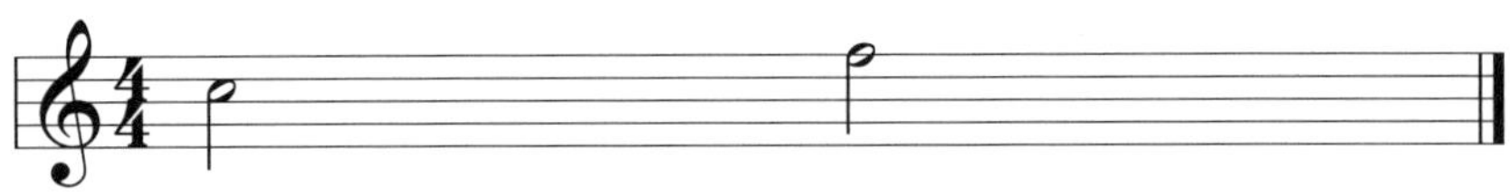

Please note: The test shown is an example. The assessor will give you a different version in the assessment.

Test 2 | Chord Recognition

The assessor will play you a sequence of chords, each with a C root note. You will hear the chord sequence twice, each time with a one measure count-in. You will then be asked to identify which chord played was major and which chord was minor. The tempo is ♩=95 bpm.

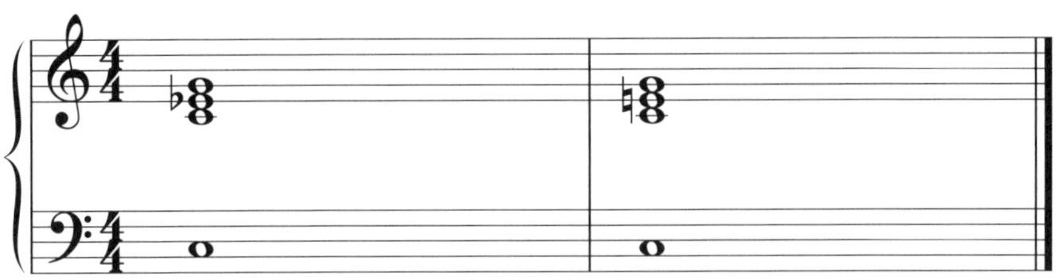

Please note: The test shown is an example. The assessor will give you a different version in the assessment.

General Musicianship Questions

The final part of your assessment is the General Musicianship Questions section, which features five questions relating to one of your choice of the performance pieces.

1. You will be asked a question relating to the harmony from a section of one of your pieces
2. You will be asked a question relating to the melody in a section of one of your pieces
3. You will be asked a question relating to the rhythms used in a section of one of your pieces
4. You will be asked a question relating to the technical requirements of one of your pieces
5. You will be asked a question relating to the genre of one of your pieces

Further guidance on the types of questions asked at this level/grade can be found at the RSL website *www.rslawards.com*

Marking Schemes

Debut to Level/Grade 8

ELEMENT	PASS	MERIT	DISTINCTION
Performance Piece 1	12–14 out of 20	15–17 out of 20	18+ out of 20
Performance Piece 2	12–14 out of 20	15–17 out of 20	18+ out of 20
Performance Piece 3	12–14 out of 20	15–17 out of 20	18+ out of 20
Technical Exercises	9–10 out of 15	11–12 out of 15	13+ out of 15
Sight Reading *or* Improvisation & Interpretation	6 out of 10	7–8 out of 10	9+ out of 10
Ear Tests	6 out of 10	7–8 out of 10	9+ out of 10
General Musicianship Questions	3 out of 5	4 out of 5	5 out of 5
TOTAL MARKS	**60%+**	**74%+**	**90%+**

Performance Certificates | Debut to Level/Grade 8

ELEMENT	PASS	MERIT	DISTINCTION
Performance Piece 1	12–14 out of 20	15–17 out of 20	18+ out of 20
Performance Piece 2	12–14 out of 20	15–17 out of 20	18+ out of 20
Performance Piece 3	12–14 out of 20	15–17 out of 20	18+ out of 20
Performance Piece 4	12–14 out of 20	15–17 out of 20	18+ out of 20
Performance Piece 5	12–14 out of 20	15–17 out of 20	18+ out of 20
TOTAL MARKS	**60%+**	**75%+**	**90%+**

Entering Rockschool Assessments

Entering a Rockschool assessment is easy, just go online and follow our simple six step process. All details for entering online, dates, fees, regulations and Free Choice pieces can be found at *www.rslawards.com*

- All candidates should ensure they bring their own Level/Grade syllabus book to the assessment or have proof of digital purchase ready to show the assessor.
- All Level/Grade 6–8 candidates must ensure that they bring valid photo ID to their assessment.

Copyright Information

Next To Me
(Craze/Chegwin/Sandé/Kumar Paul)
EMI Music Publishing Limited/Sony/ATV Music Publishing (UK) Limited/BMG Rights Management (UK) Limited

Imagine
(Lennon)
Downtown Music UK Limited

Beauty And The Beast
(Ashman/Menken)
Universal Music Publishing Limited

Lean On Me
(Withers)
Universal/MCA Music Limited

Love Yourself
(Levin/Bieber/Sheeran)
Universal/MCA Music Limited/Sony/ATV Music Publishing (UK) Limited

La Valse D'Amélie (from "Amélie")
(Tiersen)
Universal Music Publishing MGB Limited

mcps

Piano Notation Explained

THE MUSICAL STAVE shows pitches and rhythms and is divided by lines into measures. Pitches are named after the first seven letters of the alphabet.

Grace Note: Play the grace note on or before the beat depending on the style of music, then move quickly to the note it leads onto.

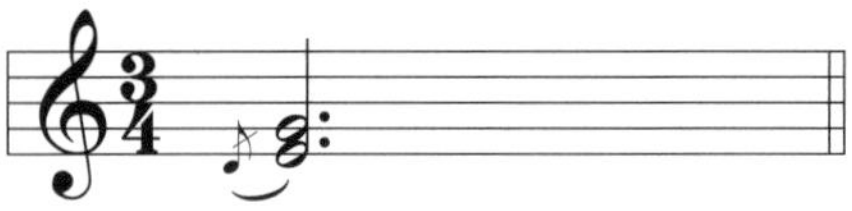

Pedal Marking: Depress and then release the sustain pedal. Multiple pedal operations in a short space of time may be simplified as shown in the last two beats of the measure below.

Spread Chord: Play the chord from the bottom note up (top down only if there is a downward arrow head). The final note should sound by the appropriate notated measure position.

Glissando: Play the notes between the notated pitches by sliding over the keyboard with the fingers or fingernails.

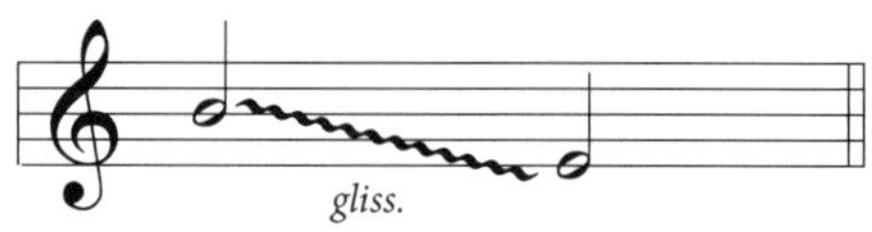

Tremolando: Oscillate at speed between marked notes.

Finger Markings: These numbers represent your fingers. 1 is the thumb, 2 the index finger and so on.

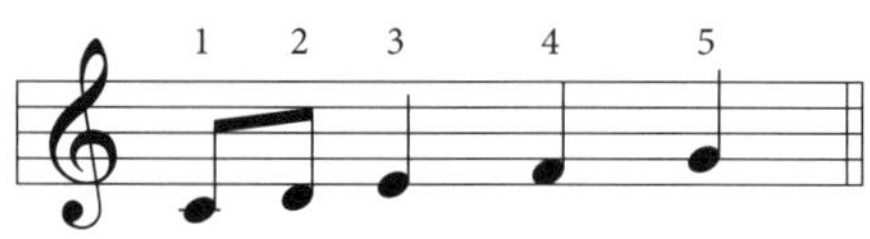

 (accent) • Accentuate note (play it louder).

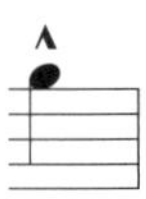 (accent) • Accentuate note with great intensity.

 (staccato) • Shorten time value of note.

 (accent) • Accentuate note with more arm weight.

D.𝄋. al Coda • Go back to the sign (𝄋), then play until the measure marked ***To Coda*** 𝄌 then skip to the section marked 𝄌 ***Coda***.

D.C. al Fine • Go back to the beginning of the song and play until the measure marked ***Fine*** (end).

Una Corda • Use soft pedal

 • Repeat the measures between the repeat signs.

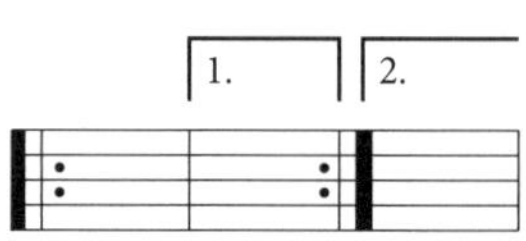

• When a repeated section has different endings, play the first ending only the first time and the second ending only the second time.